Magnificent Earth!

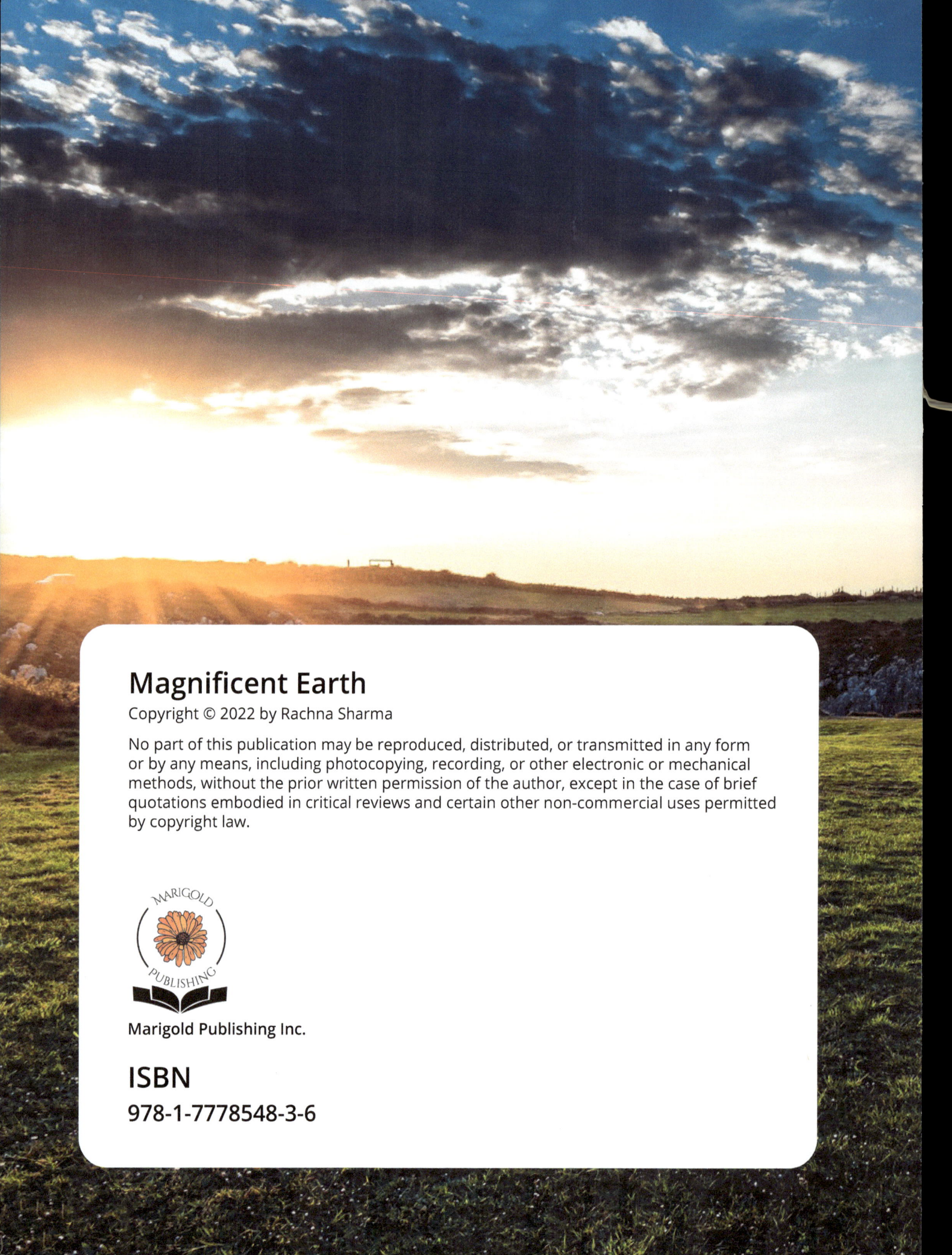

Magnificent Earth

Copyright © 2022 by Rachna Sharma

No part of this publication may be reproduced, distributed, or transmitted in any form or by any means, including photocopying, recording, or other electronic or mechanical methods, without the prior written permission of the author, except in the case of brief quotations embodied in critical reviews and certain other non-commercial uses permitted by copyright law.

Marigold Publishing Inc.

ISBN
978-1-7778548-3-6

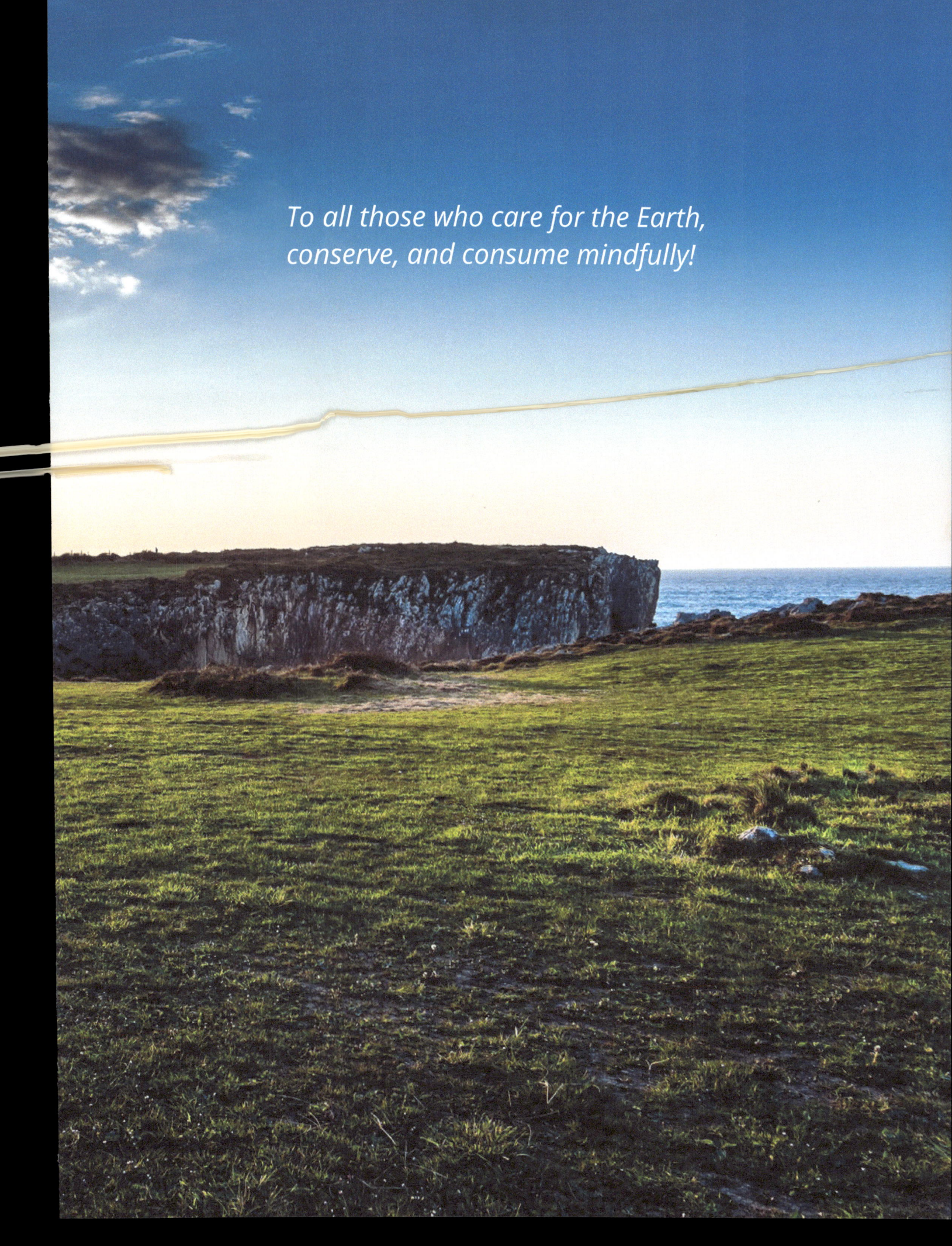

To all those who care for the Earth, conserve, and consume mindfully!

Magnificent Earth!
Mammoth, Green, and Blue.
The more you explore,
you'll fall in love, it's true!

How big is the Earth?

When ordered from the largest to smallest, Earth is the fifth-largest planet in our solar system and probably the only planet with water and vegetation. The total surface area of Earth is about 197 million square miles (510 million square km). About 71% of our planet is covered by water and 29% by land. [1]

Enduring
Accepting
Radiant
Tantalizing
Haven

Around, above and even under,
Air, soil, water, and life filled with wonder!

Home Sweet Home!

Millions of species of diverse organisms adapt to varying environments and live on Earth. So far, approximately 8.7 million species of plants and animals have been estimated by scientists. However, millions of organisms are still unknown to scientists, and only around 1.2 million species have been identified and described.[2]

Have you thought about Climate change?
Do you feel pollution in your breathing range?
The Earth's resources are in a slump,
We're quickly turning it into a dump.

How do we breathe?

Air pollution has been a growing concern. Hazardous waste is generated due to many different reasons such as mining, petroleum refining, pesticide manufacturing and chemical production. All these factors deteriorate the air quality. In addition, households also generate unsafe waste, including paints and solvents, motor oil, fluorescent lights, aerosol cans, which add to the problem and pose health challenges for people.[3]

Animals and plants,
Threatened and extinct.
Vast forests are gone,
Vanished in a blink!

Where are our homes?

According to recent estimates, the world is losing over a hundred species of plants, animals and insects every day to deforestation. Millions of hectares of forest have been altered for other uses or destroyed by natural causes. Just imagine how many animals are losing their habitats. 4

We inhale and exhale,
Share the air.
How can we ever
forget to care?

The more we want,
more factories are built.
Pollutants in the air,
with no sense of guilt!

Do you want more?

The Earth provides timber, water, fossil fuels and rocks and minerals to fulfill our needs. Still, our demands are so great that we are using those resources faster than Earth can renew them. Can we sustain it in the coming years?

Water is no different,
Splash, sprinkle, swish!
Drink, fill buckets,
or swim like a fish!

There is garbage in the water,
and giant oil spills.
Unsuitable for use,
Sealife, it kills!

Did you know?

Millions of animals are killed by plastics every year, from birds to fish to other marine organisms.
Oil spills in the ocean continue to endanger sea life. Many fur-bearing mammals lose their insulating ability and water repellency, when immersed in oil. Many birds and animals also ingest oil when they try to clean themselves, which can poison them. [5 & 6]

The food we eat
helps us to grow.
Organic is healthy,
you all must know.

Buy seasonal foods,
only local produce.
Plenty in your farms,
more than enough to use.

Does food travel?

Food travels thousands of kilometres to get from plants to our table. This long-distance transportation of food consumes large quantities of fossil fuels and generates carbon dioxide emissions.
In addition, due to the increasing demand for fresh food, food is shipped by faster and more polluting means. [7]

The forest around us,
An amazing resource!
Be mindful when you cut,
Growth takes its course.

What about forests?

Soil erosion, greenhouse gas emissions and loss of biodiversity are caused by deforestation. These issues affect not only wild plants and animals but human beings as well. Deforestation also contributes to carbon emissions. [8]

Living things on Earth,
tall, big and small.
They're all essential,
to sustain life after all!

How are we all connected?

All of the Earth's species are interdependent to survive and to maintain their ecosystems. Every living thing needs food to survive. Plants and trees produce their food from sunlight. For example, the cattle feed on the grass and then produce manure which adds nutrients to the soil to help plant growth.

A million years for
rocks and minerals to form.
They've been around
long before we were born!

Did you know?

For building and making various products, we use rocks and minerals. Unrefined materials are released when mineral deposits expose to the surface during the extraction. These pollutants can damage the health of people living near the mining site.
Due to mining, disruptions in the landscape can contribute to the deterioration of the area's flora and fauna, leading to habitat loss for microorganisms and large mammals.

Everything you use,
day and night.
Ingredients, items,
products in your sight.

Colours, shapes, sizes,
large and small.
Whatever we need,
Earth provides it all!

Think about it!

Rocks and minerals are essential to our modern society. Glass is made from melted quartz sand, and a ceramic plate is created from clay minerals heated at high temperatures. Not just that, your cell phone contains over 40 different minerals, including copper, silver, gold, and platinum. Everything that you own or use has ingredients from the Earth.

Before you consume,
Ask yourself a question.
Are you part of the problem
or part of the solution?

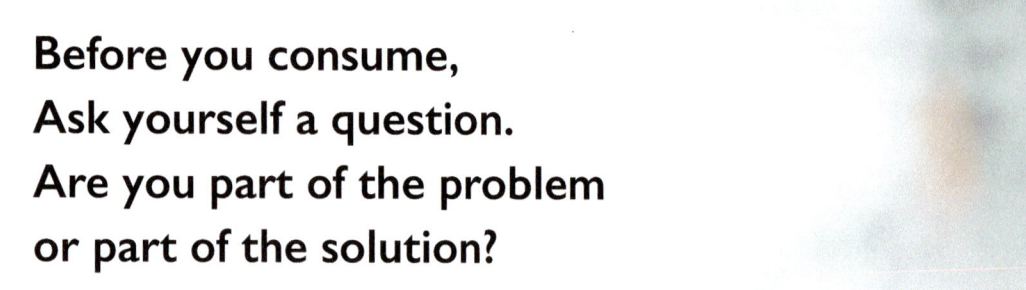

Are we mindful?

We are using more and more resources at an unsustainable rate. The extraction and processing of materials to make products, using fossil fuels, and transporting food contribute to global greenhouse gas emissions, habitat destruction, biodiversity loss, and water strain.

Stop littering.
Responsibly consume.
Live life in awareness
with nature in tune.

Every little effort of yours counts.
Together it's all going to mount!

Reduce, Reuse, Recycle!
Waste diversion helps to keep the garbage away from landfills. By reusing, recycling, composting, we save the resources and prevent waste from becoming a source of pollution. For example, recycling paper products means saving trees. Recycling metal means less mining and thereby less mining pollution.

Save water, fossil fuels,
minerals, and rocks.
Do what you can,
pull up your socks.

We can't sit back
for generations to come.
They too, will need
their families to run.

What can you do?
Using fossil fuels for energy affects the environment and also the air and water quality. Earth can not replenish fossil fuels, rocks and minerals at a fast rate.
It's time to take action, make changes to our lifestyle to make a difference. But, first, we must be mindful about how we use the Earth's resources and protect the environment for the next generation.

To create an Earth,
clean, pollution-free.
Whatever you do,
be Earth-friendly!

Stop complaining,
"What can I do alone?"
Believe in your power.
No! Don't postpone!

What can you do?

Using fossil fuels for energy affects the environment and also the air and water quality. Earth can not replenish fossil fuels, rocks and minerals at a fast rate.

It's time to take action, make changes to our lifestyle to make a difference. But, first, we must be mindful about how we use the Earth's resources and protect the environment for the next generation.

To create an Earth,
clean, pollution-free.
Whatever you do,
be Earth-friendly!

Stop complaining,
"What can I do alone?"
Believe in your power.
No! Don't postpone!

Can you take action?
To give a little hand to our planet, each year, on April 22, more people across the globe celebrate Earth Day. By picking up litter, planting trees, and increasing awareness, we try to make our world a better place to live.
It's time we think about the impact of our actions and make every day an Earth Day!

Collaborate
Brainstorm
The time is NOW!

Bring change,
Take ACTION,
Figure out HOW?

What can you do?
Everyone could make a difference in the health of the Earth. You can learn about local organizations that are working to help the environment and support them.

- Get involved.
- Consume responsibly to help save Earth's resources.
- Reduce, Reuse, Recycle!
- Learn about Eco leadership around the world; get inspired and inspire others.

Remember, every little effort counts!

Endnotes

1. Sharp, Tim. "How Big Is Earth?" Space.com, July 6, 2021. https://www.space.com/17638-how-big-is-earth.html.

2. National Geographic Society. "Biodiversity." National Geographic Society. National Geographic, June 5, 2019. https://www.nationalgeographic.org/encyclopedia/biodiversity/#:~:text=Scientists%20have%20estimated%20that%20there,most%20of%20which%20are%20insects.

3. Bradford, Alina. "Pollution Facts & Types of Pollution." LiveScience. Purch, February 28, 2018. https://www.livescience.com/22728-pollution-facts.html.

4. Hectares of forests cut down or burned. The world counts. (n.d.). Retrieved March 10, 2022, from https://www.theworldcounts.com/challenges/planet-earth/forests-and-deserts/rate-of-deforestation/story

5. Chepkemoi, Joyce. "What Is the Environmental Impact of the Mining Industry?" WorldAtlas. WorldAtlas, April 25, 2017. https://www.worldatlas.com/articles/what-is-the-environmental-impact-of-the-mining-industry.html.

6. Fisher, Matthew R, ed. "Minerals." Lumen. Lumen Learning. Accessed February 17, 2022. https://courses.lumenlearning.com/suny-monroe-environmentalbiology/chapter/minerals/.

7. Center for Urban Education about Sustainable Agriculture. (2018, February 5). How far does your food travel to get to your plate? CUESA. Retrieved March 10, 2022, from https://cuesa.org/learn/how-far-does-your-food-travel-get-your-plate

8. Cook, M. (2019, March 2). Four consequences of deforestation. Sciencing. Retrieved March 10, 2022, from https://sciencing.com/four-consequences-deforestation-7622.html

Rachna Sharma | Author

Rachna Sharma is always keen on educating kids about the environment and sustainability. Magnificent Earth is written with a hope to connect children with the Earth, provider of all and everything we need to survive. This book will encourage kids to dig deeper and find ways to consume responsibly.

She has also authored *Weirdo, When Did You Arrive?, 3D Story and My Genie*.
All these books are available on Amazon.

Rachna Sharma has been teaching for over 25 years. She has a postgraduate degree in Child Development, and currently, she lives and teaches in Ontario, Canada.

Henry K Raj | Digital Graphic Design

Henry is an artist and creative designer with more than 15 years of experience. he has worked with various industries as a creative designer and art director. His expertise in the areas of creative advertisements, magazines, illustrations, infographics & corporate presentations. Learned art and design from Kalakshetra and spreading the mythological art works and murals.

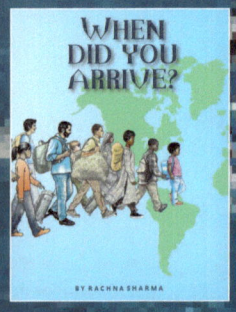
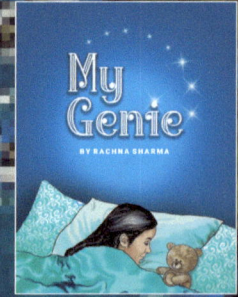

www.ingramcontent.com/pod-product-compliance
Lightning Source LLC
Chambersburg PA
CBHW042257100526
44589CB00003B/55